D1486515

The Guru and the King

Bali Rai

Illustrated by Victoria Maderna

A & C Black • London

White Wolves series consultant: Sue Ellis,
Centre for Literacy in Primary Education

This book can be used in the White Wolves Guided Reading
programme by readers of average ability in Year 2

First published 2012 by
A & C Black, an imprint of
Bloomsbury Publishing Plc
50 Bedford Square
London
WC1B 3DP

www.acblack.com

ISBN 978-1-4081-5574-5

This book is produced using paper that is made from wood
grown in managed, sustainable forests. It is natural, renewable
and recyclable. The logging and manufacturing processes conform
to the environmental regulations of the country of origin.

Printed and bound in China by C&C Offset Printing Co.

1 3 5 7 9 10 8 6 4 2

Chapter One

Jai Singh watched his mum lighting a candle.

"Why do Sikhs celebrate Diwali, Mum?" he asked.

"Because of Guru Hargobind," she replied. "He was sent to prison by a powerful king."

Jai's eyes grew wide with shock.

"Prison?" he asked. "Did he do something bad?"

Jai's mum shook her head.

"No," she replied, pointing to the table. "Sit down and I'll tell you what happened."

"Can I have some ice cream?"

His mum smiled. "Yes, Jai, but only after your dinner," she told him. "Now, the story begins in the year 1618, at Gwalior Fort in India…"

Chapter Two

After six years in prison the Guru longed to go home to his family. It was almost Diwali, and people would be lighting lamps and celebrating. But the prison was damp and dark.

"I wish we could go home," said Prince Rajesh. He was one of fifty-two princes who had also been imprisoned by the king.

Guru Hargobind smiled.

"Soon," he told the prince.

"But it isn't fair," complained Rajesh. "The King is wrong to imprison us because we disagree with him."

"Have faith," replied the Guru.

Chapter Three

The King tossed and turned in his sleep.
He dreamt of a great army attacking his
kingdom. A large black bird watched
him through the darkness. Its beady eyes
shone red.

Suddenly he sat up. Sweat dripped from his brow. His hands shook and his heart beat faster. He was scared.

"CALL MY ADVISOR!" he bellowed to his servants.

An old man arrived very quickly, holding a lamp. He looked worried and his white hair stood on end.

"You called, Majesty?" he asked, quivering with fright. The King had a foul temper.

"A nightmare," the King explained.
"Tell me what it meant – at once!"

The old man sighed. "What did you
see, Highness?"

The King told of a raven, blacker
than night, watching with fiery eyes from
the window. He described a great army
conquering his lands. Fresh beads of sweat
dripped from his face.

"It ends with a man's face. He wears a beard and a pale turban," he said. "The same face, over and over again. I've woken up shivering each night for a month!"

The old man stroked his long white beard.

"The raven is a bad omen," he explained. "It is your voice, the one in your head. It is telling you to change your ways."

15

"How so?" the King demanded.

"You must release Guru Hargobind. He has done no wrong. The longer you delay, the more danger you will face."

The King's eyes grew wide.

"And if I release this man, I will be saved?" he asked his advisor.

"Yes, your Majesty."

"Then we haven't a moment to lose!" cried the King. "I must see this Hargobind!"

Chapter Four

However, when the King met him, the
Guru refused to leave.

"HOW DARE YOU DEFY ME!" the
King shouted.

"The princes," said Hargobind quietly.
"They must be released too."

The King's face grew scarlet with anger.

"IMPOSSIBLE!" he cried.

"Then I stay," replied the Guru.

The King thought for a moment. Then he sneered.

"Very well," he said with a wicked grin. "Any prisoner who can cling to your clothing may go with you. The rest can rot!"

"Every single one?" asked the Guru.

"That's what I said!" snapped the King, stomping from the prison in a fit of rage. His advisor followed.

"But your Majesty?" the advisor whimpered.

"WHAT?"

"What of the raven and the great army?"

"BAH!" snapped the King. "It's only a dream. No one tells me what to do!"

Chapter Five

Rajesh turned to Hargobind moments later.

"We can't ALL hold onto you!" he cried. "It's impossible."

"Nothing is impossible," the Guru told him. "Gather the others. I have a plan."

When all the princes were together, Hargobind explained that they would stay imprisoned for another year. Some of them groaned. Others simply nodded. The Guru had defied the King for them. They were willing to listen.

"Each week one of us will ask the guards for a piece of string," he told them.

"Why should we do that?" asked another prince, Bhavek.

"Because in exactly fifty-two weeks from today, we shall leave this prison," the Guru told him. "All of us."

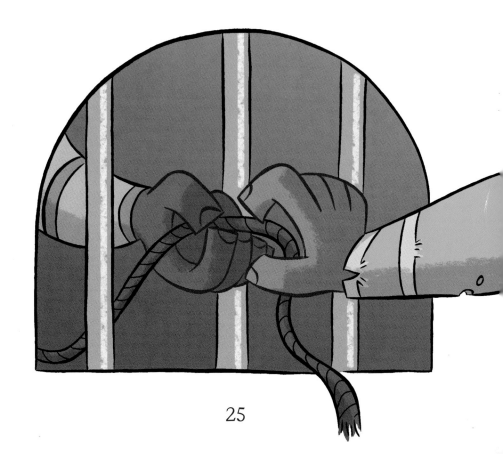

Once they heard the plan, the princes murmured amongst themselves.

"Fifty-two princes," said Rajesh with a smile. "And fifty-two pieces of string!"

The Guru smiled.

Chapter Six

One year later, the Guru asked to see the King.

"I am ready to leave, your Highness," he said. "And the princes are coming with me."

The King scoffed. After a whole year, he was no longer worried. He still had his kingdom despite the nightmares. The omens had been wrong. He also doubted that the Guru could beat his challenge.

"Remember our bargain!" the King boastfully reminded him. "Do the impossible – I dare you!"

To his amazement, that is exactly what the princes did. Fifty-two pieces of string had been tied to the Guru's tunic. Each prince held a piece.

The King was aghast but he had given his word. He had to release them. Slowly, the Guru led the princes out of the prison and into the night...

"But how did they get home in the dark?" asked Jai.

"It was Diwali," replied his mum. "Lanterns hung in every tree. Candles burned in every window. The lights led them home and that's why Sikhs celebrate Diwali too."

"That's a cool story," said Jai. "Can I have my ice cream now?"